ASK ISAAC ASIMOV ?

What is an eclipse?

Heinemann

First published in Great Britain by Heinemann Library
an imprint of Heinemann Publishers (Oxford) Ltd
Halley Court, Jordan Hill, Oxford OX2 8EJ

OXFORD LONDON EDINBURGH MADRID
ATHENS BOLOGNA PARIS MELBOURNE
SYDNEY AUCKLAND SINGAPORE TOKYO
IBADAN NAIROBI HARARE GABORONE
PORTSMOUTH NH (USA)

98 97 96 95 94

10 9 8 7 6 5 4 3 2 1

British Library Cataloguing in Publication Data is available from the British Library on request.

ISBN 0 431 07652 9

Cover designed and pages typeset by Philip Parkhouse
Printed in China

Picture Credits
pp. 2-3, National Optical Astronomy Observatories; pp. 4-5, courtesy of NASA; p. 5 (inset), Keith Ward;
pp. 6-7, E. W. Perry/Third Coast, © 1987; p. 6 (inset) Gareth Stevens, Inc.; pp. 8-11, Pat Rawlings; pp. 12-13,
courtesy of NASA; pp. 14-15, Pat Rawlings; p. 16, © George East; p. 17, Craig Calsbeck; p. 18, Gareth Stevens,
Inc.; p. 19, © Richard Baum; pp. 20-24, courtesy of NASA

Cover photograph © Science Photo Library/Kenneth W. Fink
Back cover photograph © Sygma/D. Kirkland

Series editor: Elizabeth Kaplan
Editor: Patricia Lantier-Sampon
Series designer: Sabine Huschke
Picture researcher: Daniel Helminak
Picture research assistant: Diane Laska
Consulting editors: Matthew Groshek and John D. Rateliff

Contents

Words that appear in the glossary are printed in **bold** the first time they occur in the text.

A world of questions

Our world is full of strange and beautiful things. For instance, from time to time, a dark shadow crosses the face of the Sun or the Moon. People used to think a dragon was gobbling up the Sun or the Moon. They would bang on pots and pans to scare away the dragon and bring back the light.

Today we know that such changes in the appearance of the Sun or the Moon are not caused by dragons but by **eclipses**. What is an eclipse? Let's find out.

Hide and seek

An eclipse occurs whenever one thing moves in front of another and hides it. The Sun, the Moon and even stars can be eclipsed. A cloud can pass in front of the Sun or Moon and hide it, which is a kind of eclipse. The Sun or Moon can pass behind a tall building, which is a kind of eclipse, too.

If you put your hand up in front of your eyes to shield them from the Sun, your hand is eclipsing the Sun. These are only a few examples of eclipses.

What is a solar eclipse?

When the Moon moves in front of the Sun, a **solar eclipse** occurs. During a solar eclipse, the Moon slowly passes in front of the Sun, until the Sun is almost completely hidden. Then, the Sun looks like a black circle surrounded by a halo of reddish light. The halo is really the Sun's **atmosphere** shining round the rim of the darkened Sun.

As the Moon moves past the face of the Sun, the Sun shines again. Solar eclipses only occur when the Earth, the Moon and the Sun are in a straight line.

Sun

Moon

Earth

Moon shadow

During a solar eclipse, the Moon casts its shadow on the Earth. This picture shows how the shadow might look from the Moon.

The Moon's shadow has two parts: a small dark part at the centre of the shadow, called the **umbra**, and a larger, lighter part surrounding the umbra, called the **penumbra**. From the Earth, you will see a solar eclipse if you are in either the umbra or the penumbra of the Moon's shadow.

Whole or part?

If you are in the Moon's umbra, you will see a **total eclipse** of the Sun. But if you are in the penumbra, you will see only a **partial eclipse**. In a total eclipse the Moon completely covers the Sun. In a partial eclipse the Moon hides part of the Sun. This makes the Sun look as if a notch has been punched out of its edge, as shown above.

Partial solar eclipses are more common than total eclipses. On average, a total solar eclipse will occur at a given spot on Earth only once every 350 years!

What is a lunar eclipse?

When the Earth moves directly between the Sun and the Moon, a **lunar eclipse** occurs. During a lunar eclipse, the Earth's shadow travels across the face of the Moon. The shadow blocks out the moonlight. But the Moon does not turn completely black. Sunlight passing through the Earth's atmosphere bounces off the face of the Moon. This light gives the eclipsed Moon an eerie reddish orange colour. Unlike a solar eclipse, a lunar eclipse can be seen from every point on Earth from which the Moon is visible.

14

Sun

Earth

Moon

In and out of the umbra

A total lunar eclipse occurs when the umbra of the Earth's shadow covers the Moon entirely. During the middle of a total lunar eclipse, the entire surface of the Moon darkens for an hour or two.

When only part of the umbra passes over the face of the Moon, we have a partial lunar eclipse. During the middle of a partial lunar eclipse, the Moon looks as if a chunk has been taken out of it.

17

Transits and occultations

We can see eclipses with other planets and stars. Mercury and Venus sometimes pass in front of the Sun. We call this event a **transit**. During a transit, Mercury and Venus look like tiny dots moving across the Sun's face. The pictures on these pages show Mercury passing in front of the Sun during a transit.

During an **occultation**, a **heavenly body** blocks the light from a star. Occultations often happen with double stars, which circle each other in close orbit. Sometimes one of the two stars passes in front of the other, blocking our view of the more distant star. The closer star occults, or hides, the other star.

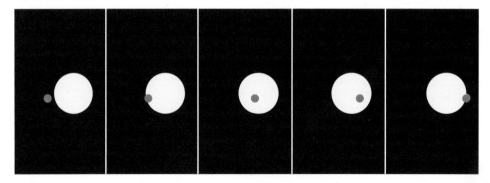

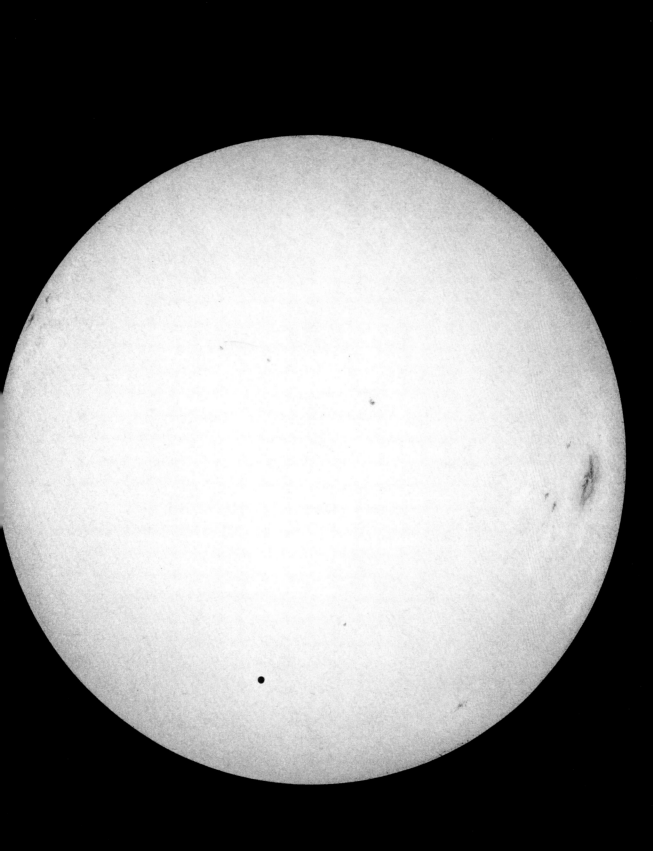

How to see an eclipse

You need a telescope to get a good view of transits and occultations. But for a lunar eclipse, you can just watch as the Moon slowly turns a reddish orange.

Solar eclipses, however, are dangerous to watch unless you take special precautions. The Sun's burning rays can damage your eyes. To watch a solar eclipse, poke a small hole in a piece of cardboard and hold the cardboard parallel to the ground. The hole will make an image of the Sun that you can project onto a smooth, light-coloured surface. Look down at the image and watch how it changes shape as the eclipse progresses.

WARNING:

NEVER LOOK DIRECTLY AT THE SUN. NEVER LOOK AT THE SUN THROUGH A TELESCOPE OR BINOCULARS.

An unearthly beauty

Which do you think would be more beautiful, a solar eclipse or a lunar eclipse? Some people think the Sun's dramatic darkening makes a solar eclipse very exciting. Other people say that the strange orange glow of the eclipsed Moon makes a lunar eclipse more haunting than the disappearance of the Sun. Most people agree that eclipses are among the most awe-inspiring events we can witness in the heavens.

Glossary

atmosphere: the gases that surround a planet, star or moon

eclipse: an event that involves the passage of an object in front of a heavenly body, so that the light from that body is blocked for a time

heavenly body: any star, planet, moon or other natural object that is found in space

lunar eclipse: an eclipse that occurs when the Earth's shadow passes over the face of the Moon; during this time Earth, the Moon and the Sun are all in a straight line

occultation: an event that occurs when a heavenly body blocks the light from a star

partial eclipse: an eclipse in which the face of a heavenly body is only partly blocked

penumbra: the light outer part of a shadow

solar eclipse: an eclipse that occurs when the Moon passes between Earth and the Sun; during this time, the Earth, the Moon and the Sun are all aligned

total eclipse: an eclipse in which the face of a heavenly body is completely blocked for a time

transit: an event during which Mercury or Venus passes in front of the Sun as viewed from the Earth

umbra: the dark central part of a shadow

Index